Jesus' Parables About Making Choices

James W. Moore

JESUS'

Parables About
Making Choices

DIMENSIONS
FOR LIVING
NASHVILLE

JESUS' PARABLES ABOUT MAKING CHOICES

This book is printed on acid-free paper.

Library of Congress Cataloging-in-Publication Data
Moore, James W. (James Wendell), 1938–
  Jesus' parables about making choices / James W. Moore.
      p.   cm.
ISBN 978-0-687-49133-9 (pbk.: alk. paper)
1. Jesus Christ—Parables.   2. Choice (Psychology)—Religious aspects—Christianity.   I. Title.
  BT375.3.M65   2007
226.8'06—dc22

2006101423

07 08 09 10 11 12 13 14 15 16—10 9 8 7 6 5 4 3 2 1

MANUFACTURED IN THE UNITED STATES OF AMERICA

*For our grandchildren (Sarah, Paul, Dawson,
and Daniel) as they grow and mature that (by
the grace of God and with the help of the
incredible teachings of Jesus)*

*they will make wise choices . . .
Choices that will be good
and right and Christ-like,
Choices that will make this world
a better place.*

CONTENTS

INTRODUCTION

Why did Jesus use parables, and how do we unravel them and discover their timeless and powerful messages? Let me begin by giving you five key ideas that help unlock the truths found in all the parables of Jesus.

First, Jesus spoke in parables—short stories that teach a faith lesson—to be understood and remembered, to proclaim the good news, and to make people think.

Second, Jesus saw himself as one who came to serve the needy, and he believed that the kingdom of God existed anywhere kingdom-deeds such as love, mercy, kindness, and compassion were being done.

Third, God's love for us is unconditional; and God wants us to love one another like that—unconditionally.

Fourth, one way to discover the central truth of a parable is to look for the surprise in it. Look for the moment when you lift your eyebrows, or the moment when the original hearers of the story probably thought or said in surprise—or maybe even shock—"Oh, my goodness, did you hear that?"

Fifth, it's important to remember that parables are designed to convey one central truth. Parables (as opposed to allegories, in which everything in the story has a symbolic meaning) make one main point.

Parables slip up on us. They flip our values. They turn our world upside down. They surprise us. This is the great thing about the parables of Jesus: They are always relevant and always personal. They speak eloquently to you and me, here and now. In this book, we will examine six of Jesus' thought-provoking parables about making choices to see if we can find ourselves, and God's truth for us, in these magnificent truth-stories. They are, after all, truth-stories for us—truth-stories from the mind of Jesus that can change our lives as they proclaim God's truth for you and me.

1

Choosing to Grow Up:
Navigating the Stages of Life

Scripture: Luke 15:11-24

Our children and grandchildren came in for the weekend a few years ago to celebrate Easter with us. On that Saturday evening we took the entire family (all ten of us) over to Goode Company Taquería for a casual, child-friendly meal.

As we walked in, we began to look at the large menu printed on the wall just above the serving line. I was pointing out to everybody that we could order hamburgers, hot dogs, steaks, or Mexican food.

Just then, our four-year-old grandson Daniel asked what was, for him, the ultimate question. In a loud voice that everybody in the restaurant could hear, Daniel said, "Does this place have ketchup?" For Daniel, that was the key question. For Daniel, that was the measuring stick for a good restaurant: "Does this place have ketchup? If they have ketchup, then it's O.K. here." By the way, in case you are wondering, Goode Company Taquería *does* have ketchup, so it is now on Daniel's list of approved five-star restaurants!

Now, let me raise a key question, a measuring-stick question, for the church. Here it is: Does the church, as a community of faith, produce spiritually mature Christians?

Let me show you what I mean. In growing up, we normally pass through three stages of life.

First, there is the childish stage, where the cry is, "Please do something for me!"

Second, there is the adolescent stage, where the cry is, "Please leave me alone. I don't need you or anybody. I can take care of myself!"

And third, there is the mature adult stage, where the cry is, "Please let me do something for you! Let me be a servant for others! Lord, make me an instrument of your love and peace and hope and healing."

Let's take a quick look together at these three stages of life and their unique characteristics.

The Childish Stage

Of course, we all love children. Life brings no greater blessing than a child. Obviously children are wonderful, but the reality is that children come into the world screaming, demanding. "Please do something for me." "Do everything for me. Hold me, rock me, talk to me, sing to me, entertain me, walk me, feed me, burp me, change me, and do it right now!"

Children *have* to do that. That's the only way they can communicate. It's the only way they can survive. And it's understandable in a child. But if a child never grows beyond that, if a child never matures, if a child never develops physically, mentally, socially, emotionally, and spiritually, it is a heartbreaking tragedy. And the sad truth is that some people do remain "childish" all the days of their lives.

Childish people are basically selfish and self-centered. They never think of the needs of others. Childish people have not yet learned how to share and care. They have not yet learned how to be grateful and generous. They have not yet learned how to be patient or polite or considerate or gracious.

Do you know anybody like that? Childish people (whatever age they may be) go through life screaming, "Please do something for me! And do it right now!" "I have this problem. What are you going to do about it? What have you done for me lately?"

The Adolescent Stage

Here, the key word is *arrogant,* but other descriptive adjectives fly fast and furious: *rebellious, restless, discontented, ruthless, prideful.* Adolescent people quite simply are those who never grew up. In trying to "cut the apron strings," they went overboard. They let the pendulum swing too far, and they have become hostile and resentful of any authority over their lives.

They are scared to death, but they try to cover that up with a false bravado, again and again loudly saying things like, "I don't answer to anybody! I'm my own boss! Nobody's going to tell me what to do or how to behave! My life's my own, and I'll do as I please! You gotta look out for number one! I'm a self-made person! I don't need anybody!"

Adolescent people say things like that so

often and so loudly that you wonder who they are trying to convince.

One biblical illustration of the adolescent stage is the picture of Adam and Eve in the Garden of Eden, saying, in effect, "Who does God think he is, telling us what we can eat and what we can't eat!"

Do you know anybody like that? The word here is *arrogant*, and the cry of the adolescent stage is, "Please leave me alone. I can take care of myself!"

The Mature Adult Stage

I don't know why somebody would give this to me, but "a friend of mine" put on my desk a description of "How to Know You're Growing Older." It reads like this:

You know you're growing older

- when everything hurts, and what doesn't hurt doesn't work;
- when you feel like the night before, and you haven't been anywhere;
- when your little black book contains only names ending in *M.D.*;
- when you get winded playing chess;
- when you join a health club and don't go;

- when you sit in a rocking chair and can't get it going;
- when your knees buckle, and your belt won't;
- when dialing long distance wears you out;
- when your pacemaker makes the garage door go up when you see a pretty girl walk by.

Now, these may be signs of growing older, but they are not signs of maturity. Growing older doesn't necessarily mean that we have become mature. Some people live a long time and have a lot of years under their belt but still have not made it to spiritual maturity. Somehow they got stuck in either the childish stage or the adolescent stage, crying, "Please do something for me!" or crying, "Please leave me alone!" On the other hand, I know some young people who haven't lived so many years, and yet they are amazingly mature.

The key word here is *love*. It is fascinating to note that both Jesus and Paul equated maturity with love. Jesus called love the key sign of discipleship, and Paul said that love is the greatest of spiritual gifts. So the measuring stick for spiritual maturity is loving compassion; humble, willing service; gracious thoughtfulness.

Love means being a servant Christian. The most mature person is the person most able to be loving, and the cry here is, "Please let me do something for you! Please let me help you! Please let me serve God by serving others. Lord, make me an instrument of your peace and grace. Lord, let me be a conduit for your love."

We see these three approaches to life expressed dramatically in the parable of the prodigal son. At first, the prodigal son childishly and selfishly demands, "Give me my inheritance now! I don't want to wait around until you die!" How presumptuous! How childish!

Then, he moves into the adolescent stage and runs away to the far country. As he walks down the road, can't you just hear him saying these arrogant words: "I'm my own boss now! I'm number one! It's all about me! I'm not answering to anybody anymore. I can make it all by myself. I don't need my father or my brother. I don't need anybody!" How arrogant! How adolescent!

But then, look what happens. The prodigal squanders his money on riotous living and ends up (of all things) a feeder of pigs, which for a Jewish boy back then was as low as it got. It was the depths of degradation. The absolute pits!

It was also the "two-by-four" that got his attention—that "grew him up." The scriptures say that "he came to himself" (Luke 15:17), which means that he matured. And then (don't miss this now), he returns home and says humbly, "Father, make me a servant. I was so foolish and so ungrateful and so presumptuous. I was so childish and so adolescent. I'm no longer worthy to be your son. Please make me a hired servant."

Now, we know the rest of the story, how the father forgave him and loved him back into the family circle, but we also see that the prodigal son grew up. He became a different person.

In these three stages—the childish stage, the adolescent stage, and the mature adult stage—we see precisely the ways in which people relate to life today, the ways people relate to the church, to marriage, to work, to school, to the nation, to others, and to God.

Let me show you what I mean with three thoughts.

First of All, Think with Me about the Church and How We Relate to It

I have been around the church a long time now, and over the years I have come to realize that these three approaches are precisely the three ways people relate to the church.

Some people relate to the church *childishly.* That is, they say, "I'll come to church as long as you please me. I'll participate as long as you let me sit where I want to sit, as long as I get the choir robe I want, as long as we sing the hymns I like to sing, as long as the preacher says what I want him to say, as long as the teacher teaches what I want taught; I'll come as long as you make me happy. But if anyone crosses me, if anyone does something I don't like, I'll quit. I'll jump on my tricycle and go home." How childish!

And then, there are some who relate to the church in an *adolescent* way. They say, "I don't need the church. I surely don't need to go to Sunday school. That's for kids and old folks, not for me. I'm going to live my life out there in the far country, doing my own thing. I have three cars and a boat. Why would I need the church? Nobody's going to tell me how to live my life, especially not the church!"

But then, thank God, there are those who relate to the church as *spiritually mature adults,* who say, "Let me be the church for others! Let me be part of the continuing ministry of Jesus Christ. Lord, make me an instrument of your amazing grace! Let me be a servant Christian. Let me do whatever needs to be done to help the cause of Christ and the church."

Second, Think with Me about Marriage and How We Relate to It

Some come to marriage in a *childish* way. They say, "I'll stay married to you as long as you make me happy. If you do what I want you to do, if you please me, if you act like I want you to act and say what I want you to say, if you make me happy, then I'll stay married to you. But if you don't, I'm going to get me another playmate." How childish!

Then, there are other people who are *adolescent* in their approach to marriage. They say, "I'll marry you, but I won't answer to you or to anybody. I want three nights out a week, with no questions asked. I don't have to answer to you, and where I go and what I do are none of your business. Nobody owns me! Who do you think you are, asking me where I've been?" How adolescent!

Then, thank God, there are some people who come to marriage like *spiritually mature people,* saying, "Let me love you. Please let me love you." And when you have two people approaching marriage like that at the same time, you have heaven on earth. Our problem is that we spend all of our time trying to find the right person to marry, rather than learning how to be the right person.

Third and Finally, Think About How We Relate to God

The gauge here is our prayer life. Be honest now: Are you *childish* in your praying? Do you come to God selfishly saying, "Lord, give me this or that. Lord, do this for me. Do that for me. Bless me. Give to me"? How childish!

Or are you *adolescent* in your approach to prayer, saying, "Prayer? Who needs it? Not me! I can make it just fine all by myself! I don't need God or anybody"? How adolescent!

But then, thank God, there are others who are *spiritually mature*, and they pray in the manner of Saint Francis of Assisi, "Lord, use me. Make me your servant. Make me an instrument of your peace. Where there is hatred, let me sow love. Where there is injury, let me bring pardon. Where there is doubt, let me cultivate faith. Where there is despair, let me instill hope. Where there is darkness, let me light a candle." Thank God for these spiritually mature adult people who pray like that and who live like that!

Now, let me conclude with two quick observations. First, please don't categorize people. Don't try to figure out who is childish, who is adolescent, and who is spiritually mature. Because, you see, the truth is, all three of these potentialities reside in every one of us at every moment. At any given moment, I have a choice—I can be childish, I can be adolescent, or I can be spiritually mature.

The second observation is that the Christian faith is saying something very simple but very profound to us, namely this: Grow up! Be mature! And the way to grow up and be mature is to learn how to be more loving, how to be a servant. That's what it is all about!

2

Choosing to Be Humble:
O Lord, It's Hard to Be Humble

Scripture: Luke 18:9-14

Over the years, I have learned something that's very important to remember, namely this: that sometimes our worst day can turn out to be our best day; that sometimes our lowest, most agonizing moment can become a stepping-stone toward spiritual maturity; that sometimes a moment of painful failure can, by the grace of God, be redeemed.

Have you ever heard someone say something like this: "That was a terrible experience, but in some ways it was the best thing that ever happened to me"? Let me show you what I mean.

It was a beautiful spring day, a day just made for playing baseball! Just a few weeks before, I had celebrated my twelfth birthday. At the time, baseball was my passion, my ambition, my life. I slept with my baseball cap on, I loved it so much.

I had a new glove, a new bat, a new ball, a new pair of cleats, and a brand-new Little League uniform. Our first game was that very afternoon at 4:00 p.m. at Hollywood Park. Our team was favored to win the league championship and to go on to the city finals.

I was primed and ready for action. I had everything needed to start the new season, except for one thing: I didn't have a plug of chewing tobacco! I had noticed on TV that some of the best Major League players always had a big chew of tobacco lodged firmly in the side of their mouth, making their cheeks puff out like they had the mumps.

I was determined to give it a try, and I was delighted later that morning when an older friend stopped by to wish me luck and to give me a big plug of chewing tobacco.

Now, my mother and father had warned me about chewing tobacco. They had said, "It's not good for you, and it will make you sick at your stomach!" I had heard their advice, and for many years I had heeded it; but now I was twelve years old, and I knew all about life (or so I thought), and I didn't think my parents really knew or understood the finer points of baseball.

So, I slipped out to the garage for my first (and last) experience with chewing tobacco. To my surprise, Mom and Dad were right: I got so sick, I must have turned green.

After an hour or so of suffering in solitude in the garage, my dad found me. Painful though it was, I told him what I had done and blurted out an apology. He hugged me and said, "You stay here. I'll go get some medicine."

My appreciation for my dad grew by leaps and bounds that day, because he not only brought me the medicine but he also never told anybody what I had done that day. The medicine worked wonders, and soon I felt better physically, but spiritually and emotionally I was a wreck.

Embarrassed, I went straight to my room and sat there in silence, ashamed, sorrowful, scared, and penitent—genuinely penitent! I fell down on my knees beside my bed and prayed more fervently than I had ever prayed before.

The words were not high-sounding or theologically distinctive, but in many ways, it was one of the best prayers I ever prayed, just repeating, "O God, I'm sorry! I'm so sorry!"

Now, that was a terrible day, one of my worst moments. I shudder to think about it, and yet, in retrospect, it was one of my *best* days, because it brought me to God; it brought me to my knees; it brought me to my senses.

That day, as never before, I learned the meaning of penitence, and through the tender way my dad handled that situation, I learned that day as never before the meaning of grace and forgiveness.

I was touched some time ago by a letter to Ann Landers, the former longtime syndicated advice columnist, written by another twelve-year-old boy. Listen to this:

> Dear Ann Landers:
>
> I am a boy who is twelve years of age. I did something my parents didn't think was right, and as punishment they made me stay home from a ball game I was dying to see. The tickets were bought and everything. They took my cousin instead of me. It was the worst day of my life.
>
> I decided they were terrible to treat me so bad, and I started to pack my suitcase to run away. I finished packing and I thought maybe I should write a good-bye letter.
>
> I wanted my folks to know why I was

running away. I got to thinking about lots of things as I was writing and decided I ought to be fair and apologize for a few things I had done that weren't right.

After I started to write I thought of lots of things that needed apologizing for. I then began to thank them for the nice things they had done for me, and there seemed to be an awful lot of them.

By the time I finished writing the letter, I unpacked my suitcase and tore up what I wrote. . . . I hope all kids who think they want to run away from home will sit down and write a letter to their parents like I did, and then they won't go.

Signed,
A Rotten Kid

Ann answered:

Dear Kid:
You don't sound rotten to me. You sound great. I wish you were mine!

You see, our bad days can turn around. Sometimes our worst day can turn out to be our best day, because sometimes our worst days are the ones that bring us to our senses—or, even better, to our knees!

We see something of this in Jesus' parable of the Pharisee and the publican. Evidently the publican—a tax collector—had had a bad day, maybe one of the worst, because he was driven by his problems to the Temple, ashamed, groping, sorrowful, beating upon his chest (catch the agony of that now), a vivid, dramatic, heart-wrenching symbol of penitence.

But Jesus tells us that this man, this painfully penitent man, went home justified rather than the other. The publican's worst day may have turned out to be his best, because his worst day brought him to God.

Remember the story with me. In Luke's Gospel uniquely, we see how much Jesus loved stories with surprise endings, and how much he loved stories where in the end the "little guy" comes out on top. We see both of those elements in this great parable.

Two men go up to the Temple to pray. One is a Pharisee, and the other is a publican, a tax collector. The Pharisee, the symbol of religious authority, marches proudly in; this is his turf; he is a big man at the Temple; he knows his way around. He goes to the most prominent spot in that sacred place to show off how pious he is. *People will be very impressed with my religiosity, and well they should be,* he reasons, and then he prays this prayer (Luke 18:11-12):

> God, I thank you that I am not like other people: thieves, rogues, adulterers, or even like this tax collector. I fast twice a week [the law demanded only one fast per week]; I give a tenth of all my income [the law required that only agricultural products be tithed].

So prays the proud Pharisee. But the tax collector, in humility and penitence, stands reverently toward the back of the Temple, far from the altar. He beats upon his chest, ashamed of what he has done, and he prays for forgiveness (Luke 18:13):

> God, be merciful to me, a sinner!

Jesus concludes the parable by saying, "I tell you, this man [the humble tax collector] went down to his home justified rather than the other [the arrogant Pharisee]; for all who exalt themselves will be humbled, but all who humble themselves will be exalted" (Luke 18:14, adapted).

It's a great story, isn't it? There is so much here to think about, but for now let me just underscore four very significant insights in this parable. Let's walk through them together.

First, Arrogant Pride Is Destructive

The Pharisee in this parable has come to symbolize arrogant pride, the opposite of humility. The scriptures tell us that he "stood and prayed thus with himself, 'Look at me, how good I am; listen to me, what all I do!' " (Luke 18:10-11, KJV, author's adaptation).

It is significant to note that in the Pharisee's prayer, God is mentioned only once; the Pharisee mentions himself four times. He emphasizes his own goodness, and he misses the grace of God, tripped up by his own arrogant pride.

One of Aesop's fables shows in a primitive, straightforward, and dramatic way the danger of this kind of pride. You may remember it. It's called "The Mice and the Weasels."

The war between the mice and the weasels had been going on for a long time. The mice were losing every battle, and after one defeat they called a meeting to discuss the situation.

"The trouble is, we are poorly organized," said one mouse.

"The trouble is that the weasels don't fight fair," said another.

"The real trouble," said a third mouse, "is that nobody is in command. What we need are leaders."

So the mice chose several leaders and named them commanders. Now, the commanders were proud of their position. They insisted on wearing decorations that would show their rank. So they put heavy medals on their chests, and they placed large gilded horns on their heads.

All went well until their next battle. The weasels won again, and once again the mice had to retreat. Most of the mice were lucky and escaped into their holes. But when the commanders tried to follow the other mice to safety, they could not get into the escape holes because of the tall, fancy horns they wore on their heads. The weasels caught these mice easily and ate every one.

The moral of the fable is obvious: Vanity costs more than it's worth! Arrogant pride is dangerous and destructive!

Now, a second insight.

Second, Our Condemning Judgments Boomerang

Our criticisms of others come back to haunt us. As someone once said, "When you point a finger at someone else, you have three fingers pointing directly back at you!"

That's the way it works. But when will we ever learn? Like the Pharisee, we look down our noses at other people, we gossip, we criticize, we condemn others, trying to make them look bad and us good, and in the very process we are the ones who come off looking bad and unattractive.

That is precisely what happened to the Pharisee in this parable. That's what happened to Martha that day when she tried to condemn her sister, Mary. That's what happened to the elder brother as he condemned the prodigal son.

When we judge other people harshly, we smudge ourselves and stain our own souls and reveal our own insecurity! Do you know why? Because our condemning judgments of others cut us off from God. The point is clear: You can't come into the presence of God with hatred in your heart. You can't love God and hate your brother or sister. You can't get close to God with bad feelings toward others in your soul.

First, arrogant pride is destructive. Second, our condemning judgments boomerang on us.

Here's number three.

Third, It's Important to Use the Right Measuring Stick

Some years ago, I was building a playhouse for our children in the backyard. One part of the project required precise measurement, but I could not for the life of me make it come out right.

Suddenly, after several frustrating attempts, I realized what the problem was: I had thought I was using a yardstick, but accidentally I had picked up a meter stick instead. My measurements wouldn't come out right because I was using the wrong measuring stick.

Now, that can happen to us spiritually. As a matter of fact, that was the Pharisee's mistake. The Pharisee measured "downward," and this always produces pride. He used the lowly publican as his measuring stick, and next to the publican, the Pharisee thought he himself looked pretty good. "Lord, I thank thee that I am not like other men, especially this publican here." The Pharisee measured downward, and that was the wrong measuring stick.

On the other hand, the publican measured upward, and this always produces humility. When we measure ourselves against the incredible perfection of God, we can only bow in humility and say, "God, be merciful to me, a sinner."

It's so important to use the right measuring stick, and the right measuring stick for righteousness is God himself.

Fourth and Finally, We Come Back to Where We Started: Sometimes Our Worst Day Can Indeed Turn Out to Be Our Best Day

Four years ago, a young man named Fred came to see me. I don't know if I have ever seen anyone more penitent than he was that morning. He was so ashamed, so remorseful, about what he had done.

He had had a drinking problem for some time. His wife had been trying for months to get him to face it and seek help, but he would always dismiss her by saying he could handle it. But then one day he showed up at work in a drunken stupor and got fired.

Angry, Fred got into his new car and, being in no shape to drive, ran it into a telephone pole, totaling the car. Fred was scraped up some, but not seriously injured.

He woke up the next morning, bruised and sore, without a job, without a car, and with a horrendous hangover, and to make matters even worse, his wife was quietly crying as she and the children packed to leave him.

It was the lowest moment of Fred's life; the pits! A few hours later he showed up at the church. Over the next few days, weeks, and months, he began the process of facing up to his drinking problem. And now with the help of the church; with the help of a recovery program; with the help of his wife and children, who came back to him; and with the help of God, Fred is whipping his problem.

He knows that he is still an alcoholic; he knows that he is just one drink away from big trouble. But taking it one day at a time, he hasn't touched a drop in four years. Recently he came back to see me to celebrate four years of sobriety, and as we talked about that terrible day four years ago when he lost everything, he said, "You know, as I think back on it, I realize now that that horrible day was the best day of my life, the best thing that ever happened to me. I know it sounds strange to say that, but it brought me to my senses, it brought me to the church, it brought me off the bottle, it drove me to my knees, and it brought me back to God!"

Arrogant pride is destructive. Our condemning judgments of others boomerang and come back to haunt us. It is important to use the right measuring stick. And our worst day can, by the grace of God, turn out to be our best day.

That's what Jesus teaches us in this powerful parable. In this colorful story, he shows us that humility is a much better choice than pride.

3

Choosing to Listen:
Do You Need a Hearing Aid?

Scripture: Mark 4:1-9

Have you ever had this experience? Has something like this ever happened to you? You walk up to somebody you know and say, "How are you doing? How are things going for you?" Then the person answers with something like this: "Well, I lost my job last week. My wife left me. I haven't been able to sleep lately because of my asthma. My daughter fell this morning and broke her arm in two places. And my son got kicked off the football team yesterday! *That's* how things have been going for me lately." And before you realize it, you say, "Oh, that's great!" Have you ever had that happen to you? Sometimes we respond without really listening, and therefore we respond incorrectly or improperly. We do that with people all the time, but even worse, we do it with God. We close our ears to him. We don't hear him. We don't listen, and consequently our response sometimes is all wrong.

Do we hear God when he speaks to us? He is speaking to us loud and clear, you know, through people and events all around us; and if we have the mind of faith, the heart of faith, and the ears of faith, we can hear him. Once we have heard him, then we can respond properly. But so often, we don't hear God. We tune him out, close him out. We turn a deaf ear to him.

Dr. Ira Williams, in his book *God in Unexpected Places*, dramatically captures in a series of brief vignettes the way we turn a deaf ear to God. Listen closely to his words. He titles this "It's Only God."

> Molly Jones relayed the purpose of her call to the freckle-faced boy who answered the doorbell. Unless she found a few more mothers to work in the classroom, they wouldn't be able to hold Vacation Church School. She knew how much the sessions meant to the children and hoped Mary Smith would help.

Tommy went to get his mother, but she looked up from her movie magazine and whispered, "Tell Molly I'm not feeling well—I'll call her later."

But what she really said was, *Never mind—it's only God. He can wait.*

Jeanie Smith came into the den where her dad was reading the sports page and brought her church school workbook. In one section of the lesson, the father is supposed to help his child read the scripture selection and answer some questions. Joe Smith turned aside from the paper long enough to say, "Jeanie, can't you see I'm busy?"

But what he really said was: *Never mind—it's only God. He can wait!*

The pastor made a luncheon appointment with Mack Tucker. He laid before the businessman some crying needs of a deprived neighborhood in the shadow of their church. Mack leaned back in his chair and shook his head. "Preacher, are you still on that do-gooder kick? I thought you had something important to talk about."

But what he really said was: *Never mind—it's only God. He can wait!* (Ira Williams, *God in Unexpected Places* [Nashville: Abingdon Press, 1974], pp. 83-84)

You see, God is speaking to us loud and clear, and the question before us now is, can we hear him? Can we hear God speaking to us through people, through events, through life situations?

That is precisely what this parable in Mark 4 is about. Jesus is underscoring the importance of hearing God's Word and responding properly. Remember the parable with me.

The sower went out to sow his field. Some seed fell on the path but couldn't grow because the ground was too hard. Some seed fell on rocky soil; and because the ground was shallow, the plants sprang up quickly, but then quickly died away because they had no roots, no depth. Some other seed fell among the thorns; and there the plants tried to grow, but the thorns choked the life out of them. Still other seed fell on good soil, and this seed grew and yielded a great harvest.

Now, these four different soils represent for us four different ways in which people hear and respond to the seed of God's Word. Let's look at them together and see if we can find ourselves (or someone we know) somewhere between the lines.

First of All, Some of the Seed Fell on the Path

The path soil was hard and crusty, and it just did not receive the seed at all. There are people like that—people who are hard, cynical, callused, self-centered, crusted over, closed-minded. These people won't listen. They hold God at arm's length, at a safe distance. They will not let him or his Word penetrate their lives.

The "Path Person" is anybody who has a closed mind and will not let God's Word in. The cry of the Path Person is, "We never did it that way before!" The Path Person is like the man who celebrated his one hundredth birthday and said, "I've seen lots of changes in my time, and I've been against every one of them!"

In the *Peanuts* comic strip, Lucy is a Path Person. One day Linus is trying to get through to her. He says, "Lucy, you and I are brother and sister. We ought to get along. We ought to love one another. We ought not to bicker and fight all the time." Lucy totally ignores him; she doesn't even look up.

In the next frame, Linus goes out and says the same thing to a brick wall. "Lucy, you and I are brother and sister. We ought to get along and love one another." No response there either. Then Linus turns to Charlie Brown. "You are right, Charlie Brown! You're right! Talking to Lucy is just like talking to a brick wall!"

I think my favorite *Peanuts* cartoon of all time is that one where Violet (a character similar to Lucy) is chasing Charlie Brown and shouting, "I'll get you, Charlie Brown! I'll get you! I'll knock your block off!" All of a sudden, Charlie Brown screeches to a halt and turns and, in a very mature way, says, "Wait a minute! Hold everything! . . . If we, as children, can't solve what are relatively minor problems, how can we ever expect the nations of the world to . . ." And then, POW! Violet slugs him and says, "I had to hit him quick . . . he was beginning to make sense!"

You know, that is exactly what the Path People of the first century did to Jesus. They "hit him quick," because he was beginning to make sense! He was bringing a new message, some new ideas, some changes. And he was a threat to their closed minds, so they hit him quick with a cross.

People with closed minds are still nailing Jesus to a cross.

He speaks "love," but they will not listen.

He cries "new life," but they will not respond.

He commands, "Follow me," but they will not obey.

He says, "Learn of me," but they say, "Sunday school is for kids!"

The Path People are hard, callused, crusted-over people. They have ears, but they will not listen or respond because they live in the prison of the closed mind.

Second, We Come to the Rocky-Soil Hearers

The Rocky-Soil Hearer represents the person who is shallow. He or she hears, becomes enthusiastic, responds immediately, but then fades away quickly because there is no depth, no roots. The rocky soil was a thin layer of fertile soil on a thick layer of rock. Because the soil was shallow and fertile, the plant would immediately sprout up. But since it had no way to get its roots down deep (because of that layer of rock), the plant would just as quickly shrivel and die. The plant could have no staying power, no endurance, no lasting life, because there was no depth, no strong roots.

Many people respond to God like that. They get momentarily religious. They get emotionally stirred up. They get excited, but they never put their roots down, they never get deep into it, and their shallow faith shrivels and withers and dies. I'm thinking of a woman I used to know who got saved every September. Every September, the church would have a revival. She got "religion" every September, and it lasted until about October. She sprang up quickly every fall, but she never quite got her roots down.

I'm thinking of that couple I talked to not long ago who said they wanted to get married. But strangely I had the feeling that what they really wanted was to go on a honeymoon, and I wondered if they were really ready for that day-to-day, deep, long-haul commitment it takes to make a marriage work. Many people are like that in their faith experience: They want to have an exciting "honeymoon" in the faith, but they are not really ready for the deep, strong, tenacious commitment.

I'm thinking of the man who came to Jesus in the Gospel of Luke saying, dramatically, "I will follow you wherever you go!" But Jesus turned him away. Why? We don't know all the details, but evidently Jesus sensed that this man was a Rocky-Soil Hearer who had no depth; who did not understand the cost of discipleship or the commitment required; who did not comprehend the obedience demanded or the allegiance needed to handle the pressures that loomed just ahead in Jerusalem, in the shape of a cross. The Rocky-Soil Hearers sound good, they talk a good game, but they have no depth, no roots, and they soon wither away.

I'm thinking of that Sunday morning in New York City some years ago, when a woman came to Dr. Henry Sloane Coffin after the morning service, shook his hand warmly, and said, "Oh, Dr. Coffin, you just don't know what a help your sermons are to my husband since he lost his mind!" Too often this is the assumption—namely, that faith has nothing to do with the mind, that Christianity and thinking are poles apart. Nothing could be farther from the truth.

A disciple is by definition a *learner*. Jesus said, "Love God with your mind!" That's what theology is. That's what Christian education is. That's what Sunday school is about—loving God with our minds; hearing, heeding, studying, discussing, and growing in God's Word. We often hear people cry out for more emotion in our religion. I understand that, and I sympathize with that, but let me say that for every person who has left the heart out of his or her faith, I know two dozen others who have left the *head* out—who have left the mind out, who have left out the intellectual commitment that is so important in putting our roots down and growing a deep, stable, strong faith.

The Rocky-Soil Hearers are shallow. They can get stirred up, but they have no depth. They have ears, but they do not hear the full demands of God's Word; and after a while, they shrivel up and wither away because they don't have any roots.

Third, Look at the Thorny-Soil People

The Thorny-Soil People are the people who get their priorities mixed up. Some of the sower's seed fell among thorns. It was good soil, but it gave all of its energy to the thorns instead of the seed. Lots of people have that problem. They give all of their attention, energy, and effort to all the wrong things. They come to church *if and when* it's convenient. They sing in the choir *if and when* it's convenient. They teach Sunday school or work with the youth *if and when* it's convenient.

Bishop Gerald Kennedy once told about a man in Los Angeles who called a church to say that he had just had an incredible spiritual experience, and that he had made the most important decision of his life: He wanted to come down and join the church on Sunday. Later, he called back and said, "I can't make it this Sunday. Something has come up." But then the next day he called back and said he could be there after all, "because the Lakers are playing out of town this Sunday!" Now, I love sports as much as anyone, but sometimes we need to get our priorities in order and remember the things that really matter.

The Thorny-Soil People are unable to put God first. They have ears, but they water down the Word and choke the life out of it until it has no real meaning for them.

Fourth and Finally, There Are the Good-Soil Hearers

The Good-Soil Hearers are the people who receive God's Word into their lives and work with it to bring forth new life everywhere. Not long ago I was driving to a speaking engagement in East Texas and listening to the Houston Astros and New York Mets baseball game on radio. At first, the broadcast was coming in loud and clear. But then there was static, and later it faded out altogether. Why? Because

I had gotten too far away from the station! Good-Soil Hearers are those who stay close to the station.

Now, let me conclude with two quick observations. First, notice that this is a tricky parable. When we look at it, we are tempted to categorize other people: "Well, Joe is a Path Person; and Betty is a Rocky-Soil Hearer." "Tim is a Thorny-Soil Person; and, of course, I am Good Soil."

That's what we tend to say, but that misses the point. The point is that within you and me at any given moment reside all four of these potential soils. At any given moment, we can be closed-minded or shallow, or we can get our priorities mixed up. Or we can be good soil and receive God's Word into our lives, and work with it to bring forth new life.

The message is clear: Be good soil! Be good listeners! Receive God's Word! Love God with your minds! Stay close to the station! And stay tuned in!

The final observation is that this is a good news parable. Notice how it ends—with a great harvest. Although three of the four soils are bad, and only one of them is good, the result is a great harvest. That's good news! We don't have to worry about the harvest. That's God's business. We don't have to worry about being successful. All we have to do is to be faithful!

So, the message is clear: Be patient! Don't get discouraged! Keep on receiving the Word and sowing the seed no matter how unpromising the situation may look, and trust God to bring a great harvest!

4

Choosing to Help:
The Three Approaches to Life

Scripture: Luke 10:25-37

In the golden days of the settling of the West, you will remember, of course, that one of the major means of public transportation was the stagecoach. But did you know that in stage-coach days, they had three different kinds of tickets you could buy—first class, second class, and third class?

A first-class ticket meant that you got to sit down. No matter what happened, you could remain seated. If the stagecoach got stuck in the mud or had trouble making it up a steep hill, or even if a wheel fell off, you remained seated, because you had a first-class ticket.

A second-class ticket meant that you got to sit down until there was a problem, and then you had to get off the stagecoach and stand to the side until the problem was resolved. You stood to the side and watched somebody else fix the problem. When the situation was corrected, you could get back on the stagecoach and take your seat, because you had a second-class ticket.

A third-class ticket meant that you got to sit down until there was a problem, and then you had to get off and push! You had to put your shoulder to it and help solve the problem if you had a third-class ticket.

As I thought about this recently, I realized something: I realized that these are precisely the ways in which people relate to the church.

Some think they have a first-class ticket, and they just sit there and expect to be catered to and waited on and pampered.

Others think they have a second-class ticket. They ride along until there is a problem. Then they bail out and become detached spectators. They get off, stand to the side, and watch somebody else fix it.

Still others (and thank God for them) think they have a third-class ticket. They ride along until something goes wrong, and then they get off and push! They address the problem creatively, they work on the situation productively, and they help fix it. They give their energy to the immediate task of solving the problem. They roll up their sleeves and get the job done.

Now, these three ways of relating to the church are really not so new. They are as old as the Bible itself. In fact, they were so pronounced in the time of Jesus that one of his most famous parables was told to address that situation. This is what the parable of the good Samaritan is all about.

The priest and the Levite in the story thought they had "privileged tickets."

- They didn't want to get their hands dirty.
- They didn't want to get mud under their fingernails.
- They didn't travel "tourist," much less third class.

They were special people, important people, holy people. They didn't need to get smudged up by the problems of the world. "Let someone else see to it." That was their motto.

But, on the other hand, the good Samaritan realized that he had a third-class ticket, so when he encountered the problem, he knew exactly what he was supposed to do: get off and help solve the problem, put his shoulder to it and bring healing, roll up his sleeves and go to work.

That's what third-class ticket holders do.

- They don't mind dealing with the difficulty.
- They don't mind getting their hands dirty.
- They don't mind taking a risk or getting involved.

That goes with the territory when you have a third-class ticket.

By the way (don't miss this now), that's what made the good Samaritan "good," wasn't it? That was indeed his goodness! He was willing to help, anxious to heal, eager to serve, ready to live, and quick to address the problem.

He was bold enough to deal with the problem in a creative, redemptive way.

- He didn't just sit there and let someone else see to it.
- He didn't just stand off to the side and watch and critique how others were dealing with the difficulty. He didn't play "the blame game"!

- No! He felt responsible—he felt called to help—and he addressed that troublesome situation lovingly in the Spirit of Christ, and that's why to this day, we call him the good Samaritan.

Third-class ticket holders are indeed good people to have around. Jesus taught us that not only here in this parable, but also in many other places. Again and again he said it. He said, "I am among you as one who serves" (Luke 22:27); "Go and do likewise" (Luke 10:37). "Those who act privileged will be last, but those who serve will be first! Those who rush to the front and act exalted will be called down, but those who are humble servants will be lifted up" (Matthew 19:30; 20:16, author paraphrases).

"I am among you as one who serves"; that was the mind-set of Jesus. Time and again, we hear him saying it, and we see him doing it.

Remember early on how he went out into the wilderness to think through the meaning of his life and the method of his ministry. *What kind of Messiah would he be?* That was the question he was grappling with! And he was tempted to claim a first-class ticket. He was tempted to go the route of power and pleasure and privilege, but no! Instead, Jesus chose the way of the suffering servant. He chose a third-class ticket.

Once he made that choice, look at what Jesus did next. He went directly to the synagogue and read aloud to the people what was to become the theme of his life. Go look it up—you'll find it in Luke 4. Here's what Jesus read to "trumpet in" and "jump-start" his ministry:

> The Spirit of the Lord is upon me,
>   because he has anointed me
>   to bring good news to the poor.
> He has sent me to proclaim release to the
>   captives
>   and recovery of sight to the blind,
>   to let the oppressed go free.
>   (Luke 4:18)

Now, what was Jesus saying? Simply this: "No privileged seat for me! I have accepted a third-class ticket, and now I'm going to tackle these hard problems!"

In the life and ministry of Jesus, we see something very, very important, namely, this: that God gives us a first-class love, but a third-class ticket. When troubles come, when difficulties arise, when problems emerge, we have to "get off and push," we have to roll up our sleeves and go to work—if, that is, we want to live in the Spirit of Christ.

Now, let me be more specific. Let's bring this closer to home as we look directly at these three mind-sets, these three ways of relating to the church and to life, and see if we can find ourselves somewhere between the lines.

First of All, Look with Me at the First-Class Ticket Mind-set

Some folks in the church act as if they have a first-class ticket. They just sit there, and they expect to be catered to and waited on. "Let someone else do the dirty work! Not me!" is their cry.

The largest McDonald's restaurant in the world opened some years ago in Moscow, the capital city of Russia. It seats more than seven hundred people. Projections were that this one restaurant would bring in approximately fifteen million dollars a year, and it is doing that. The Russian people are rushing to McDonald's for a "Bolshoi Mac."

Now, it's interesting to me that many of the Russian people who have dined under the golden arches in Moscow say that it's not the Western food that impresses them so much, but it's the way the employees cater to them.

"May I help you?"

"What can I do for you?"

"What would you like?"

"May I serve you?"

"Please enjoy your meal!"

"Have a nice afternoon."

"You deserve a break today," all said with a lilt in the voice and a warm, caring smile.

The Russian people were not used to that. But most of us are! We expect to be pampered when we go to a restaurant, and if we are not treated with excellent service, we are very disappointed. It's part of what we call our "cater culture," and that's fine. We all enjoy that.

However, we have to be careful not to let that "cater culture" mind-set cloud our understanding of the real purpose of the church. We join the church to become not God's privileged people, but God's servant people; not God's pampered people, but God's workforce.

Recently I read about a man who got to the point where he no longer could help out around the house. He told his wife that he was physically unable to work around the house anymore. She sent him to the doctor. The doctor gave him a complete physical and then later came in with the results.

The man said, "Doc, I can take it. Just tell me the truth. Give it to me straight."

The doctor said, "Well, in plain English, there is nothing wrong with you. You're just lazy!"

The man thought for a moment and then asked, "Could you give me a medical term for that, so I can tell my wife?"

Some years ago, I wrote a book with the title *Standing on the Promises or Sitting on the Premises.* The truth is that some people relate to the church with this "sitting on the premises" mind-set. They sit lazily on the premises, because somehow they have gotten in their minds the mistaken notion that they have a first-class ticket. So, no matter what happens, they just sit there and expect somebody else to do the work and cater to them.

Now, let's move on to point two.

Look Next with Me at the Second-Class Ticket Mind-set

Have you ever noticed that some folks relate to the church as if they have a second-class ticket? That is, they ride along enjoying the journey until there is difficulty or a problem. Then they bail out, stand to the side, and become detached spectators.

Now, while these second-class ticket holders

stand there watching others working hard to solve the problem, there is an added temptation, the temptation to become a "Monday-morning armchair quarterback"; the temptation not just to watch, but to criticize and gossip about the way the situation is being handled.

"They're doing that all wrong!"

"Would you look at that?"

"They don't know anything!"

"That group couldn't organize a two-car parade!"

"If you ask me, I wouldn't do it like that!"

That's the way the spectator mind-set works: "Let's find somebody to blame this on!" They stand and watch. They talk and critique and blame, but they don't help!

Like the priest and the Levite, they move quickly to the other side, thinking they have no responsibility to address the problem. "I don't want to get involved, so I'll stand to the side and wait until somebody else fixes this."

But this is not the Christian response to trouble, is it? Certainly not! This is not how our Lord taught us to deal with difficulties, is it? As a matter of fact, this way of relating to the church and to life is, at best, not helpful—and at worse, it's even dangerous.

Let me show you what I mean. As you know, many classic pieces of literature came out of the terrible days of the Holocaust in World War II. The words of Dietrich Bonhoeffer, Anne Frank, Viktor Frankl, and other great people of faith have moved and inspired millions of people all over the world for quite a few years now. Do you remember that poignant and wonderful piece written by Martin Niemöller? Niemöller was a German Lutheran pastor who was arrested by the Gestapo and sent to a concentration camp in Dachau in 1938. Amazingly, he survived the prison-camp experience and was set free by the Allied troops in 1945. Out of that horrible experience, Niemöller wrote these haunting words:

> They came for the Jews, and I didn't speak up because I wasn't a Jew.
> Then they came for the trade unionists, and I didn't speak up because I wasn't a trade unionist.
> Then they came for the Catholics, and I didn't speak up because I was a Protestant.
> Then they came for me, and by that time no one was left to speak up.
> (Quoted in the New England Holocaust Memorial)

The point is clear: We can't bail out or run away; we can't detach ourselves and stand to the side; we can't ignore the troubles of the world; we can't just wait around expecting someone else to roll up his or her sleeves and correct the situation for us.

If we are to live in the Spirit of Christ, we have to face the problems and deal with them redemptively.

That Brings Us to the Third-Class Ticket Mind-set

In our families, in our businesses, in our nation, and especially in our church, how we need people who are willing to work, anxious to help, ready to love, and eager to serve! How we need people who are determined to be part of the solution rather than part of the problem! How we need people in the church and in the world who are "quick to get out and push" when we get stuck in the mud!

Some years ago, a minister friend of mine was talking to a man about joining the church, when the man said, "I want to join the church because I want to be fed." My friend answered, "Well, that's fine, but we would all be better off if you would take off your bib and put on an apron!"

Well, how is it with you right now? Be honest; what kind of ticket are you holding right now? The Scriptures make it crystal clear through the life and teachings of Jesus Christ that God gives us a first-class love, but a third-class ticket!

5

Choosing to Try:
Failure Is Not to Try

Scripture: Matthew 25:14-29

Let me begin with three quick stories. Watch, if you will, for the common thread that runs through them.

The first story comes from the great British minister Leslie Weatherhead. When Dr. Weatherhead was a young man working his way through college, he took a job one summer as a door-to-door salesman. He had many memorable experiences that summer, but the one he remembered most vividly was one that saddened him greatly, namely, the family who met him at the door and said coldly, "Son, you are wasting your time here, 'cause we ain't interested in nothing!"

The second story comes from the pen of the noted Austrian novelist Franz Kafka. In one of his novels, Kafka tells a parable about a man who waited all his life outside a door. He looks at the door wistfully and longs to enter it. He watches the doorkeeper and wonders how to get past him and through the door. For some time, he plots and strategizes ways to get around the doorkeeper and move through the door. He schemes and plans but is afraid to try. Finally he gives up, tired, disappointed, and disillusioned.

In the end, as the man is dying, he says to the doorkeeper, "Why? Why did you keep me out?"

"I didn't," answers the doorkeeper. "As a matter of fact, this is your door, and I am here to serve you."

"But why did you stand in my way?" asks the dying man. "Why did you block me?"

"I didn't," replied the doorman. "I would have been more than glad to open the door for you, but you never asked to come in."

The third story comes from history. Some years ago in South America, Peruvian sailors were cruising up the Amazon River when they came upon a strange sight. A Spanish ship was at anchor in the middle of the wide Amazon River, and all of the crew members were lying weakly on the deck of the ship. As the Peruvian sailors drew closer, they saw that the Spanish sailors were in serious trouble. They were in terrible physical condition. They looked awful, like the picture of death itself. Their lips were parched and swollen and dry. The Spanish sailors were indeed dying of thirst.

"Can we help you?" shouted the Peruvians. The Spaniards cried out, "Water! Water! We need fresh water! We are dying of thirst!" The Peruvian sailors, surprised at their request, told them to lower their buckets and help themselves.

The Spanish mariners had thought they were lost and doomed in the open ocean. They had thought the water around them was undrinkable. So they had given up hope. They had quit trying. They had just dropped anchor and lain down to die. They were dying of thirst when, as a matter of fact, they were a couple of miles up in the mouth of the fresh waters of the Amazon River. They had been anchored there for days. For days, they had been in the midst of fresh water, and they didn't know it, they didn't discover it. You know why? Because they had given up and quit trying.

Now, of course, the thread that runs through these stories is the problem of apathy. *Apathy* means quitting on life. It is the opposite of faith. It is the opposite of hope. It is the opposite of love. It is the opposite of commitment. To be apathetic, according to *Roget's Thesaurus* (1911), is to be "spiritless," "heartless," and "sluggish." It is to be "numb," "paralyzed," and "insensitive"; to be apathetic is to be "unconcerned," "unimpressed," "unexcited," "unmoved," "unstirred," and "untouched."

I saw a bumper sticker the other day that read, "If I were concerned about anything, I would really be upset about apathy."

We all dread the thought of failure; but worse than trying and then failing, is not trying at all. Apathy is not trying at all, and it is the worst failure of all. If you try and fail, at least you know that you are alive; you are still in the game. But not trying at all means that you have quit on life, that you are numbered among the "walking dead."

The silent tragedy of life is that many people reach the point of death only to find that they never really lived; they never really loved; they never really tried. Somewhere along the way (and often quite early) they got hurt or scared or disappointed, and they quit. They refused to try anymore. Terrified by the risks and pressures and demands of life and of commitment, they pulled back into their shell and hid.

Jesus told a parable about this kind of quiet tragedy. We call it the parable of the talents. Since a "talent" was a large sum of money, a more contemporary name for this parable might be the parable of investments. Like all of Jesus' parables, this one has a simple narrative, yet it is profound in its implications.

The parable is about a businessman who decided to take a trip. The man had three associates with whom he left his fortune. To these three men, he parceled out his holdings. To one, he gave $50,000 in silver; to another, he gave $20,000; and to still another, he gave $10,000. The businessman instructed the men to work with the money, to use the money, to invest it for an appropriate return and profit.

Some time later when the businessman returned from his travels, he called in his associates for a report. The first two men had invested their money and had done quite well, and they were commended for a job well done. But the third man had been afraid, and apathetically he had done nothing but hide the money in the ground. His lack of imagination and lack of effort cost him dearly. Not only did he miss out on a promotion, but he lost all of the money, and he lost his position as well.

Apathy is so costly. Jesus shows us that in this parable. He also exposes, in this graphic story, the perfect formula for failure! Let me show you how that could be outlined.

First of All, the Servant Failed Because He Didn't Appreciate What He Had

Can't you just hear him complaining, "I didn't get as much as the others. I didn't get as much as they did. It's not fair! How can I hope to compete with them? It's not right, so I won't play the game. I'll show 'em; I won't participate at all"—the sounds of bitterness and apathy and ingratitude.

In effect, he got $10,000 before inflation, but he didn't appreciate it. In fact, he may well have resented it, because in his mind, what he had paled in comparison to the others who had more. One of the big problems we have in life is lack of appreciation.

A few summers ago, we went with our youth choir to England. We stayed in the homes of local people, and we noticed that many of the people we visited lived in such a frugal way but seemed so grateful for what they had. It made me almost ashamed of the many, many things we have, and how so often we show signs of not being grateful.

Ingratitude leads to apathy, and apathy, as we already have seen, is the worst failure of all.

J. Wallace Hamilton, in his book *Ride the Wild Horses*, tells a wonderful story about how easy it is to take for granted what we have. It's about a farmer who had lived on the same farm all his life and was tired of it, bored with it. He had inherited the farm from his father, but now he desperately craved a change. He subjected everything on the farm to his own blind and merciless criticism.

At last, he decided that he would sell the old place and buy another more to his liking. So he listed the farm with a real-estate agent, who at once came out and looked over the property, and the two men prepared a sales advertisement for the newspaper. Before giving the ad to the newspaper, however, the agent read to the farmer the ad's very flattering description of the farm: "Beautiful farmhouse, ideal location, excellent barn, good pasture, fertile soil, up-to-date equipment, well-bred stock. Near town, near church, near school. Good neighbors."

"Wait a minute," said the farmer. "Read that over again, and take it slow." Again the description was read: "Beautiful farmhouse, ideal location," and so forth.

"Changed my mind," said the farmer. "I'm not gonna sell. All my life I've been looking for a place just like that!"

Can't we relate to that? That farmer was living in a paradise, and he didn't know it.

Dr. Russell Conwell's great lecture "Acres of Diamonds," which he gave more than six thousand times, was built around this idea, the idea that the riches of life are all around us, wherever we are, but so often our eyes fail to see them for the simple reason that we magnify the difficulties, overlook the advantages, and fail to see the good in what we have.

The servant in Jesus' parable had this problem, and often—too often—so do we. He failed first because he didn't appreciate what he had. We fail like that too, don't we?

Second, the Servant Failed Because He Didn't Accept What He Had

Jesus' parable reminds us that we don't always determine the size of our talents; that is, there are certain "givens" in life. There are some things that cannot be changed. There are certain givens that we have to learn to live with that will not budge and cannot be altered. All the bitterness in the world will not change the fact that this man received a sum comparable to $10,000, or one talent. That's what he was given; that's what he needed to work with. No matter how much work or energy we give to the process, it is just a fact that there are some things in life, in your life and in mine, that will not be changed. Life has limits that we must learn to accept.

One writer suggested that this is partly what the story of Adam and Eve is about. Remember how God placed them in the garden and gave to them incredible possibilities. They could name the animals and subdue them, they could till the earth, they could enjoy all the wonderful works of nature, and they could feast on the fruit of the land. Indeed, Adam and Eve could do everything, except one thing. They had only one limitation: They were not to eat of the fruit of *one tree* in the midst of the garden.

It's almost as if this is a reminder that we are not God; we have some limits on our lives. There are some things we cannot do and some things we cannot change!

- Those of us who are 5 feet, 11 inches tall cannot be 6 feet, 5 inches.
- Most of us will never run a four-minute mile or become Miss America.

- Most of us will never be famous or the most beautiful or geniuses.
- We cannot control the Law of Gravity.
- We cannot call back cruel words already spoken.
- We cannot change our past; we cannot add a cubit to our stature.
- We cannot stop the aging process, and we cannot eliminate death.

I could go on and on pointing out numerous things in our lives that we cannot change. The real question is, how do we respond to these "trees" in the midst of our garden?

Some people spend their lives running away from them. That's what the one-talent servant did in the parable. He tried to run away and hide. He hid the money in the ground to escape the pressure.

Some people go through life playing the "if only" game: If only I were taller, if only I were smarter, if only I had married someone else, if only I had never married at all, if only I had gone to a different college, if only I had that house or that car, if only I had been born rich, if only I had more than $10,000 to work with.

The "if only" game doesn't work. It only causes us to fail to face reality. Some people resent the limitations and become bitter, cynical, and miserable.

The Christian answer is the serenity of acceptance, even the redemption of our disabilities. This is what Jesus was doing in the garden of Gethsemane. "Father, I don't want this cup, but if I must, I will drink it. Thy will be done!" (from Matthew 26:39).

Sure, the servant who had been given one talent had less than the other two, but he had enough. He had enough to do something good, something meaningful, something creative, something productive. But you know the story: He did nothing. Because he wouldn't accept what he had, he did nothing. I wonder how often that happens to us?

The servant failed, first of all, because he didn't appreciate what he had; and second, because he didn't accept what he had.

Third, the Servant Failed Because He Didn't Use What He Had

I have a friend I wish I could introduce to you. His name is Bret. At twenty years of age, if Bret were standing here beside me, he would not come up to my waist. I'll never forget the first time I saw him. He was eight years old, a third-grader at his elementary school. He was running in some races during the school's Field Day. I was so impressed by Bret's spunk and spirit. His competitors were so much larger than he was, so he didn't have much of a chance to win. I saw him run in three races that day, and in every one of them he finished last. But his mother stood at the finish line and waited for him. She would run and hug him and say, "Bret, you did real well, and I'm so proud of you!"

By the end of the day Bret had not won a single ribbon. But if I had had some Olympic gold medals, I would have put one on Bret, and one on his mother. Bret won the heart of everyone there, because he did his very best. He tried his hardest, he used what he had, and he gave his all.

Now, on that same day, there was another little boy the same age as Bret, sitting under a tree pouting, because he remembered that the year before he didn't win a blue ribbon. So this year he decided that rather than run and risk not winning first prize, he just wouldn't run at all. Rather than risk failure, he wouldn't try at all. The teachers were pleading with him to try, his mother was pleading with him to try, the other students were pleading with him to try, but he just sat there all day and pouted, and never got in the game at all.

Bret didn't win a blue ribbon, but he was a winner that day, and he still is. He's in college, drives a car, has a job, and smiles at everybody he meets. And everybody he meets loves him, because he uses what he has.

We often put off using what we have. The late Leo Buscaglia was an author and a university professor. At the start of the semester each year, he would assign a paper instructing students to respond to one question: "What would you do if you had only five days to live?" Student responses were interesting: "I would say 'I'm sorry'"; "I would say 'I love you'"; "I would say 'thank you' to my parents"; "I would set right a broken relationship." The students would turn in their papers, but when they got them back, they would find that the papers hadn't been graded. Instead of grading them, the professor had written in bold letters across the top: "Why don't you do it now? What are you waiting for?" (Leo Buscaglia, *Living, Loving, and Learning* [New York: Holt, Rinehart and Winston, 1982])

I have often wondered, when I read this parable of Jesus, whether this one-talent servant maybe was trying to get up the nerve to do something, and his employer came back before he was ready.

Procrastination—what a problem that is for us! Leo Buscaglia also spoke of this in his book *Living, Loving and Learning.*

> A girl wrote a poem she calls "Things You Didn't Do." In the poem the girl reminisces about her life with her boyfriend. She recalls how patient he was with her. She remembers
> —how she borrowed his car and dented it;
> —how she forgot to tell him the dance was formal;
> —how she flirted with some guys just to make him jealous;
> And how each time she thought he would get mad and drop her . . . but he didn't.
> He kept on loving her and forgiving her and treasuring her.
> And then she concludes the poem saying that there were so many things she wanted to make up to him when he came back from Vietnam . . .
> But he didn't

Don't wait. Do it now. If you have a word of love that needs to be expressed, say it now. If you have a broken relationship that ought to be set right, don't let the sun go down tonight without setting it right. If you have something you need to be doing, get to it; don't put it off.

The one-talent servant failed because he didn't appreciate what he had, he didn't accept what he had, and he didn't use what he had. It's the perfect formula for failure—the seeds of apathy.

6
Choosing to Prepare:
When Crisis Comes, Will You Be Ready?

Scripture: Matthew 6:25-33; 25:1-12

Some time ago, our family attended a college football game. We sat in the stands near a good friend who was watching the game with his nine-year-old son. Casually I asked the nine-year-old, "Jon, where is your little brother tonight?"

With a sheepish grin, he replied, "He's at home, packing!"

"Packing?" I responded. "Is he going on a trip?"

"No, not really," Jon answered, still grinning. "He says he's running away from home because he didn't get to come to the ball game. We only had two tickets!"

Isn't that something? A seven-year-old packing to run away from home because big brother got to go to the big game, and he didn't! I guess all little boys have moments like that. Of course, Jon's little brother didn't really run away. It was dark outside, and besides that, it's hard to run away when you are not permitted to cross the street!

I remember another incident that was similar. Some friends of ours have a son named Paul who is quite a character. When Paul was five and a half years old, he got upset one day and decided to run away, but he wanted his mother to help him pack. She went along with his little game, knowing he wouldn't go far, and together they fixed up a small suitcase with a few clothes and toys and some peanut-butter sandwiches, and Paul left.

About fifteen minutes later, a woman from down the street called. She was quite concerned as she excitedly exclaimed, "Mrs. Harris! Mrs. Harris! Your son Paul is over here, and he has a suitcase, and he says he is running away from home!" Before Paul's mother realized how it was going to sound, she blurted out, "I know, I know! I helped him pack!" Now, wouldn't you know that the woman calling had no children of her own;

there was no way she could understand that scenario!

Out of these two life vignettes, I want to point our thinking not in the direction of running away, but of packing, and packing in preparation for a journey. That's what this parable in Matthew 25 is all about. The wise bridesmaids planned ahead and took along what they would need. But the foolish bridesmaids were indeed "foolish." They didn't anticipate a problem. They didn't count on a delay. So, they didn't bring extra oil for their lamps, and that mistake came back to haunt them. They didn't plan ahead, and consequently, when the crisis-moment came, they were not prepared to face it. They had not packed the right things!

I read recently of a young bride who on her honeymoon went to the mountains with no shoes but the high heels she had on when she left the wedding. She left in such a hurry that she forgot her walking shoes. Have you ever tried to hike in the mountains in high heels?

Some years ago, I was privileged to go on a trip to the Holy Land. When our group left, it was warm here in Houston. I knew also that it would be warm in Jerusalem and Bethlehem and Cairo, so I didn't bother to take an overcoat. But there was one thing I didn't count on.

It was January, and we had to change planes in New York, where it was ten below zero and snowing. We stood outside in the frigid elements for twenty minutes waiting for a bus to take us to our departure terminal, and over and over I said through chattering teeth to concerned friends, "Oh no! I'm not cold!" I did learn something, though: It's hard to sound macho when your teeth are chattering!

That was one time I didn't pack enough, but my problem is usually the reverse. I usually pack too much! I think it is probably because I don't plan ahead. I run in at the last minute and just start grabbing things to take along with very little forethought and very little planning.

Now, that brings us to one of the central theological problems of our time, namely, what to take along on our life's journey! We have trouble trying to decide what to take along and what to leave behind, what to carry and what to unload, what is really necessary and what is extra luggage, what is essential and what is excess baggage.

Some of the great minds of history have wrestled with this problem, and all have come to the same important conclusion, namely, that we need to travel light! Remember how Jesus put it in the Sermon on the Mount. He said,

"And which of you by being anxious can add one cubit to his span of life? . . . Therefore do not be anxious about tomorrow" (Matthew 6:27, 34 RSV). Seek first God's kingdom and his righteousness, and everything else falls into place (Matthew 6:33, paraphrased).

What Jesus is really saying here is simply this: Travel light! Decide early on what is important to you, what really matters to you, and give your energies to those things. We can't do everything. We can't take everything with us on this life journey. So we have to choose; we have to decide what is essential and take that with us, and leave behind all the rest.

Well, the question then is, what do we pack? What do we include in our baggage? What do we take along? Let me suggest three things that we all need to take with us down the road; three powerful ideas that will keep our lamps of faith lit; three strong themes that Jesus underscores repeatedly and dramatically in the Sermon on the Mount.

First, We Need to Take Along a Sense of God's Watchcare Over Us

Go back and read the Sermon on the Mount (Matthew 5:1–7:29). One of the beautiful threads woven into the tapestry of that sermon is Jesus' unbending belief that God the Father is with us, that God the Father cares for us, that God the Father is watching over us. This is why Jesus says, "Don't worry so much. Don't be so fretful. Don't be so anxious. God is watching over you. Just give your energies to serving him and doing the best you can, and he will bring it out right." Remember how the hymn writer put it: "Be not dismayed, whate'er betide, / God will take care of you."

Now, some people are afraid of the future. They want as little change as possible. There's a story about a group of people who gathered at the Hudson River some years ago to see the launching of the first steamship. Out of the crowd one man was heard to say in a cynical tone, "They'll never get her going!" But they did. The steamship started up and moved out fast. Then, the same man was heard to say, "They'll never get her stopped!" We are oh, too familiar with such skepticism.

It is said that some years ago, the noted scientist Dr. Wernher von Braun was speaking on the subject of putting a man on the moon. When his lecture was over, he made the mistake that many speakers make; he asked if there were any questions. Immediately a woman's hand shot up. When Dr. von Braun called on her for her question, she said, "Why can't you folks forget about putting people on the moon, and just stay home and watch television like the good Lord intended for you to do?"

We are afraid of the unknown. The future has always been threatening and foreboding to some people. The good news is that God the Father is with us, that God the Father watches over us, and nothing, not even death, can separate us from him. As the old gospel song puts it, "We know not what the future holds, but we know who holds the future."

I ran across a beautiful little story recently that makes the point. A little boy was trapped on the second floor of a burning building. His father on the ground below called out for him to jump. It was dark, and the little boy called out in a frightened voice, "But, Dad, I can't *see* you!" "I know," said the father, "but I can see *you*, and I will catch you, so trust me and jump!" The little boy jumped into the safety of his father's strong and dependable arms.

One thing we need to take along with us for sure on our life's journey is a sense of God's watchcare over us; what serenity and poise and confidence and strength come from this! The "oil" of God's fatherly watchcare will keep our lamps aglow.

Second, We Need to Take Along with Us a Sense of God's Challenge to Us

Another significant thread that runs dramatically through the Sermon on the Mount is the challenge to do better, the challenge to be better, the challenge to try harder. Look at the challenge of the Beatitudes: *Be pure in heart . . . be merciful . . . be peacemakers . . . hunger and thirst for righteousness.* Later, Jesus challenges us to extend the law beyond outward acts. He challenges us to apply it inwardly—"even if you think it in your heart," he says. What a challenge! (See Matthew 5:28.)

And speaking of challenges to be better, Jesus says, "Go the second mile"; "turn the other cheek"; "love your enemies"; "pray for those that hurt you"; and then, the ultimate challenge: "Be perfect as your Father in heaven is perfect!" (Matthew 5:41; 5:39; 5:44; 5:48, paraphrased).

God watches over us, but he also challenges us to be better. There's a story about a Sunday-school teacher who was teaching her children's class the parable of the Pharisee and the publican. She showed the children how prideful, how haughty, how arrogant the Pharisee was as he prayed, "God, I thank you that I am not like this publican." Then, totally missing the point, at the end of class the teacher said, "Now, class, before we go, let's bow our heads and thank God that we are not like this old Pharisee!"

It's not our calling to look down our noses at other people. Our calling is to see Christ as our Savior but also as the measuring stick for our righteousness. Christ is the standard. He is the model. He is the challenge!

We need to travel light. And in our luggage, we need, first, a sense of God's watchcare over us; and second, a sense of God's challenge to us to be better.

Third and Finally, We Need to Take Along with Us a Sense of God's Ultimate Victory for Us

Again, the ring of God's victory is in the Sermon on the Mount. There we see the "blessed assurance" that God will ultimately win, and if we build our house on that solid foundation, the victory will be ours as well. Through faith, we too can have the victory.

This is why Jesus could march triumphantly to the cross. This is why Paul could endure the hardships, the persecution, the difficulty, and the misunderstanding. This is why Luther could say boldly, "Here I stand; I can do no other. God help me." This is why John Wesley could say of the early Methodists, "Our people die well," because they knew—as we can know, as people of faith—that God is on both sides of the grave. God will not forsake us or desert us. He has a victory for us.

At the very end of his book *The Morning After Death,* Dr. L. D. Johnson tells the moving story of a nineteenth-century Congregational minister of New England. His name was John Todd. He had been left an orphan when he was six years old, and then reared by an aunt, who enabled him to finish Yale College and go on to seminary. Some years later, while John Todd was pastor at Pittsfield, Massachusetts, he received a tender letter from his dear aunt, who was by that time quite old and very ill. In fact, she told him in that letter that she was in great distress. Her doctor had told her that she was terminally ill, that she had an incurable disease, and that she would die very soon.

So she wrote John, her nephew. He had been to college and to seminary; he had read and studied and was very wise. "Could he tell her about death? Was there anything to fear?"

This was John Todd's answer:

> It is now thirty-five years since I, a little boy of six, was left quite alone in the world. You sent me word you would give me a home and be a kind mother to me. I have never forgotten the day when I made the long journey of ten miles . . . to your home in North Killingworth. I can still recall my disappointment when I learned that instead of coming for me yourself you had sent your [servant-man] Caesar to fetch me. I can still remember my tears and anxiety as, perched on your horse and clinging tight to Caesar, I started for my new home.

Then John Todd described his anxiety as darkness fell before he reached his aunt's home, and how he wondered whether his aunt would have already gone to bed. He wrote that soon, however, they rode into a clearing, and sure enough, there was a candle in the window. His aunt stood at the door. He remembered how she ran to greet him and wrapped her arms around him, lifting him gently from the horse.

She had fed him supper beside the fire in the

hearth, and had taken him to his room and sat with him until he fell asleep. "You are probably wondering why I am now recalling all these things to your mind," John added.

> Some day soon God will send for you, to take you to a new home. Don't fear the summons, the strange journey, the messenger of death. At the end of the road you will find love and a welcome; you will be safe in God's care and keeping. God can be trusted—trusted to be as kind to you as you were to me so many years ago. (L. D. Johnson, *The Morning After Death* [Nashville: Broadman Press, 1978], pp. 146-47)

You see, we can travel light, with three essential things to take along, three important oils to keep our faith-lamp aglow: a sense of God's watchcare over us, a sense of God's challenge to us, and a sense of God's ultimate victory for us!

That's the message of the Trinity. God the Father always watches over us, God the Son saves us and challenges us to be better, and God the Holy Spirit (through faith) gives us the victory!

But please don't miss this: The oil was there for the foolish bridesmaids all along; they just forgot to take it with them. Don't let that happen to you. God has these wonderful gifts for us—his watchcare, his challenge, and his victory, but we have to accept them into our lives through faith.

SUGGESTIONS FOR LEADING A STUDY OF *JESUS' PARABLES ABOUT MAKING CHOICES*

John D. Schroeder

This book by James W. Moore examines six of the parables told by Jesus to see what we can learn from them about making choices. To assist you in facilitating a discussion group, this study guide was created to help make this experience beneficial for both you and members of your group. Here are some thoughts on how you can help your group:

1. Distribute the book to participants before your first meeting and request that they come having read the brief introduction and

the first chapter. You may want to limit the size of your group to increase participation.

2. Begin your sessions on time. Your participants will appreciate your promptness. You may wish to begin your first session with introductions and a brief get-acquainted time. Start each session by reading aloud the snapshot summary of the chapter for the day.

3. Select discussion questions and activities in advance. Note that the first question is a general question designed to get discussion going. The last question is designed to summarize the discussion. Feel free to change the order of the listed questions and to create your own questions. Allow a set amount of time for the questions and activities.

4. Remind your participants that all questions are valid as part of the learning process. Encourage their participation in discussion by saying that there are no "wrong" answers and that all input will be appreciated. Invite participants to share their thoughts, personal stories, and ideas as their comfort level allows.

5. Some questions may be more difficult to answer than others. If you ask a question and no one responds, begin the discussion by

venturing an answer yourself. Then ask for comments and other answers. Remember that some questions may have multiple answers.

6. Ask the question "Why?" or "Why do you believe that?" to help continue a discussion and give it greater depth.

7. Give everyone a chance to talk. Keep the conversation moving. Occasionally you may want to direct a question to a specific person who has been quiet. "Do you have anything to add?" is a good follow-up question to ask another person. If the topic of conversation gets off track, move ahead by asking the next question in your study guide.

8. Before moving from questions to activities, ask group members if they have any questions that have not been answered. Remember that as a leader, you do not have to know all the answers. Some answers may come from group members. Other answers may even need a bit of research. Your job is to keep the discussion moving and to encourage participation.

9. Review the activity in advance. Feel free to modify it or to create your own activity. Encourage participants to try the "At home" activity.

10. Following the conclusion of the activity, close with a brief prayer, praying either the printed prayer from the study guide or a prayer of your own. If your group desires, pause for individual prayer petitions.
11. Be grateful and supportive. Thank group members for their ideas and participation.
12. You are not expected to be a "perfect" leader. Just do the best you can by focusing on the participants and the lesson. God will help you lead this group.
13. Enjoy your time together!

Chapter 1
Choosing to Grow Up

Snapshot Summary

1. We need to relate to the church as spiritually mature adults.

2. Spiritually mature people approach marriage by learning how to love.

3. Spiritually mature Christians are servants and ask God to use them as instruments of peace.

Reflection / Discussion Questions

1. Name some traits and behaviors of childish people.

2. Share a time when, as an adult, you acted in a childish manner. What caused you to act that way?

3. Describe the behavior of people who are in an adolescent stage.

4. What do adolescent people lack? What do they need in order to mature?

5. Explain why love is a key word for the mature adult stage.

6. Why is growing older not always connected with maturity?

7. Describe what it means to be spiritually mature.

8. How does a person relate to the church in a spiritually mature manner? Give some examples.

9. Give some examples of what it means to have a healthy perspective regarding marriage.

10. According to the author, "Our problem is that we spend all of our time trying to find the right person to marry, rather than learning how to be the right person." Discuss that comment, and share your own views and perspectives.

11. Explain how prayer life is an indication of spiritual maturity.

12. How did your reading and discussion of this chapter personally enrich you? What additional insights or questions would you like to explore?

Activities

As a group: Create a list of choices that a person needs to make each day. Rank your choices in order of their importance, and talk about your results.

At home: Identify and reflect upon the childish or adolescent traits in your life that you would like to eliminate. Set some goals for making better, more spiritually mature life choices.

Prayer: *Dear God, thank you for the privilege of being able to make my own choices and decisions each day. Help me make wise choices that further your kingdom and help others. Open my eyes to childish ways and help me to be a more mature Christian. Amen.*

Chapter 2
Choosing to Be Humble

Snapshot Summary

1. Arrogant pride is destructive.
2. Our condemning judgments often boomerang back upon us.
3. It's important to use the right measuring stick.
4. Sometimes our worst day can turn out to be our best day.

Reflection / Discussion Questions

1. Explain what it means to be humble, and give an example.
2. Share an experience you've had in humility that was a stepping-stone toward maturity.
3. Give some reasons why it's hard to be humble.
4. Compare and contrast the attitudes of the Pharisee and the publican. How was each man's attitude reflected in his prayer?
5. Name some signs or symptoms of arrogant pride.
6. Explain why condemning judgments often boomerang or come back to haunt us.

7. Give some reasons why people make condemning judgments. Rather than judging others, what is a better course of action to take?

8. In what way did the Pharisee use the wrong measuring stick?

9. Give some examples of how we often use the wrong measuring stick today.

10. Share a time when the grace of God turned a bad situation into something good.

11. How does it feel when a worst day suddenly becomes a best day?

12. How did your reading and discussion of this chapter personally enrich you? What additional insights or questions would you like to explore?

Activities

As a group: Design a spiritual measuring stick. Instead of numbers, use words that describe Christian traits. Discuss the value of measuring your spiritual growth.

At home: Practice humility this week at home and in public. Become more aware of your words and actions, and how they affect others. Be a humble servant.

Prayer: *Dear God, thank you for showing us the value of humility. May we choose to be humble rather than being arrogant or judgmental. Help us look only to you as the measuring stick for our words and deeds. Amen.*

Chapter 3
Choosing to Listen

Snapshot Summary

1. Some people fail to hear and respond to God's Word because their mind is closed.

2. Some people fail to hear and respond to God's Word because they are shallow and have no depth.

3. Some people fail to hear and respond to God's Word because they are unable to put God first.

4. People who listen, hear, and respond to God's Word are enabled to work with it to bring forth new life everywhere.

Reflection / Discussion Questions

1. Share a time when you made a response without really listening.

2. What are some reasons why people sometimes turn a deaf ear to God?

3. How is attentive listening a choice?

4. What makes a person a good listener? Share some listening tips.

5. In what ways does God speak to us in a loud and clear voice?

6. Why does a "path person" fail to hear and respond to the seed of God's Word?

7. Discuss the author's observation that a disciple, by definition, is a learner.

8. In your own words, describe what it means to be a "rocky-soil person."

9. How are "thorny-soil people" different from rocky-soil people?

10. Speaking for yourself, why do you most often fail to hear and respond to God's Word? What helps you personally to be a good-soil hearer?

11. What lessons can be learned from this parable?

12. How did your reading and discussion of this chapter personally enrich you? What additional insights or questions would you like to explore?

Activities

As a group: Make a list of obstacles that prevent effective listening. Then make a second list of keys to effective listening. Compare and contrast the two lists.

At home: Reflect upon your own listening skills. How can you become a more effective listener? Put your ideas into practice throughout the week.

Prayer: *Dear God, thank you for the gift of listening. Open our ears and our hearts to the words and needs of others. Help us learn to listen and then act. Increase our listening skills so that we may hear your Word and serve you well. Amen.*

Chapter 4
Choosing to Help

Snapshot Summary

1. Some people go through life expecting to be catered to and waited upon.

2. Some people go through life watching others fix problems.

3. Some people go through life using their time and talents to fix problems.

Reflection / Discussion Questions

1. Share a time when you chose to help and felt good about the experience.

2. Name some reasons why people steer clear of getting involved.

3. Discuss why people choose to help individuals and organizations in need. Are some reasons better than others? Explain.

4. What are some of the attitudes and beliefs of "third-class ticket holders"?

5. Why do you think the parable of the good Samaritan is so well known?

6. What lessons can we learn from the parable of the good Samaritan?

7. What do people with first- and second-class mind-sets miss out on?

8. In your view, why do some people have a servant attitude, while others do not?

9. In the church and in the community, what's the best strategy for helping people with first- and second-class ticket mind-sets to become third-class ticket-holders?

10. When you are asked to help, what criteria do you use to make a decision?

11. What expectations do you believe Jesus has for his followers today?

12. How did your reading and discussion of this chapter personally enrich you? What additional insights or questions would you like to explore?

Activities

As a group: Discover how much your help is needed. Using current local newspapers, find opportunities to help others. Cut out the opportunities you find and paste them together to create "Help Wanted" poster. Discuss the wide range of opportunities you discovered, and take steps to volunteer your time and talents to help.

At home: Look for and take advantage of an opportunity to be a "good Samaritan" at home and in public this week.

Prayer: *Dear God, thank you for the good Samaritans in this world. Help us look for and accept opportunities to help those in need. Open our eyes to burdens we can lift and ways we can give of ourselves. Amen.*

Chapter 5
Choosing to Try

Snapshot Summary

1. We need to appreciate what we are given.
2. We need to gladly accept what we are given.
3. We need to use what we are given.

Reflection / Discussion Questions

1. Describe what it means to be apathetic, and give an example.
2. According to the author, why is apathy the worst failure of all?
3. What are some of the fears people have that can trigger apathy or inaction?
4. What are some cures for apathy?
5. How does it feel to be unappreciated?
6. When we fail to appreciate others, what problems are created?
7. Why is it important to accept our limitations and the fact that there are some things in life we can't change?
8. Share a personal limitation you have learned to accept.

9. What are some of the reasons why people fail to use what they are given?

10. Share a time when you lost out because of procrastination.

11. Share a time when you overcame doubt or the fear of failure and were rewarded because of the effort you made.

12. How did your reading and discussion of this chapter personally enrich you? What additional insights or questions would you like to explore?

Activities

As a group: Discover the talent within your group. Let each person list one talent they have and at least three ways to use it. Share your lists with the group.

At home: Reflect upon your life to identify a worthwhile project or opportunity you have not followed through on due to procrastination, apathy, fear of failure, or some similar reason. Take a step out in faith this week toward accomplishing what needs to be done.

Prayer: *Dear God, thank you for the many talents we are given. Help us appreciate, accept,* and use our talents to help others. Rid our hearts of apathy, and give us the hearts of servants. Amen.

Chapter 6
Choosing to Prepare

Snapshot Summary

1. We can live with a sense that God is with us.
2. We can live with a sense of God's challenge to us.
3. We can live with a sense of ultimate victory.

Reflection / Discussion Questions

1. Compare and contrast the wise bridesmaids and the foolish bridesmaids in the parable.
2. Share a time when you anticipated the need to be prepared.
3. What are some reasons why people might fail to properly prepare for difficult times?
4. Name some ways in which attending church prepares us for life.

5. Share a time when you felt God's presence.

6. If you have a sense that God is with you, how does that make you feel?

7. In times of crisis, how can we be reminded of God's presence?

8. What are some tools of faith that help us cope with life?

9. Talk about important areas in life (for example, one's personal finances, automobile, or place of residence) in which people should be prepared, and share ideas on what people could do to prepare.

10. In what ways, and for what reasons, does God challenge us?

11. How do we all share victory in Christ? What does that mean for us in our lives today?

12. How did your reading and discussion of this chapter personally enrich you? What additional insights or questions would you like to explore?

Activities

As a group: Reflect on and discuss what it means to "travel light" in life. Make a list of things you'll need in order to travel light, and make a list of things you definitely will not need.

At home: Reflect on your personal sense of God's watchcare over us, God's challenge to us, and God's ultimate victory for us. Pray, asking God to give you the guidance and wisdom you need in order to be prepared, and also the trust and confidence you need so that you won't be anxious about tomorrow.

Prayer: *Dear God, we are so grateful for the ultimate victory you have achieved in Jesus Christ. Thank you for being with us always, and in all things. Grant us the tools we need to be your faithful servants and to meet life's challenges in readiness. Amen.*